\

remember

**from my time
on earth**

What I
remember
from my time
on earth

poems

PATRICIA YOUNG

Anansi

Published in 1997 by
House of Anansi Press Limited
1800 Steeles Avenue West, Concord, ON
Canada L4K 2P3

Distributed in Canada by
General Distribution Services Inc.
30 Lesmill Road
Toronto, Canada M3B 2T6
Tel. (416) 445-3333
Fax (416) 445-5967
e-mail: Customer.Service@ccmailgw.genpub.com

01 00 99 98 97   1 2 3 4 5

Canadian Cataloguing in Publication Data
Young, Patricia, 1954–
What I remember from my time on earth
Poems.
ISBN 0-88784-592-4
I. Title.
PS8597.O673W42 1997   C811'.54   C97-930113-0
PR9199.3.Y68W42 1997

Cover design: Pekoe Jones
Printed and bound in Canada
Typesetting: ECW Type & Art, Oakville

House of Anansi Press gratefully acknowledges the support
of the Canada Council and the Ontario Arts Council in
the development of writing and publishing in Canada.

for P. K.

Contents

3

1

Even the Brilliant Chimpanzees

In the Chinese restaurant we drink
Tsing Tao beer and choke down
words, handful by handful.
We grow quiet in the name
of our fervent desires.
Sometimes it is easier to exist

in silence. What other
eloquences have we learned
in two million years?
At Olduvai Gorge someone picked up
the sliver whacked off a rock,
peeled words from the other's

tongue like peeling rind
from a freshly picked melon.
Outside, the streets are ancient
gullies roaming the badlands of Tanzania.
But we do not huddle in wet misery, no, we are
smarter than that, have just enough sense

to come inside where these vermilion
walls hold back the elements
as we try to hold back
primitive emotion. Darling,
we are old, much older
than the grunts and squawks

sprouting from the buds at the end
of our spinal cords, older even
than the dried-up riverbed Leaky discovered —
that twenty-five mile long gash
in the earth's surface. Tonight
it is your mammalian brain

that bowls me over, that beautiful
cantaloup ripening beneath your skull.
And if we were to climb up
on the table between us,
go for each other
smelling of ginger root and lime

would the sky
cease pouring its grief
into every crevasse? When it rains
even the brilliant chimpanzees
fold their hands over their heads
in little caps of shelter.

The Wall

Once I climbed a wall in a dream.
Like the dream of flying —
that same effortlessness
and ability to overcome
the usual limits of the bones.

Took my skill for granted.
With agility and speed
I lizard-clambered to the top.

It did not sadden me
that only I
could scale that vast cliff.

The wall is not a metaphor.
I would not mislead you.

In life I make mistakes
but in the dream
my hands and feet held on
with an insect's grip.

It rose before me, a blank sheet
entering heaven. To climb
was all I lived for.

From a great height I looked down.
Your upturned face was inscrutable
as a white-washed surface.

I knew I would not fall.

The wall was what it was
and clung to me like a lover.

The Origins of the Kiss

I wish to speak of origins:
the snail's caress, its antennae and the roots
growing deep in the earth.
I wish to speak of the duck's bill,
guillemots nibbling each other's
feet, the pose of any feathered thing.
I have traced the kiss to Semitic antiquity,
beyond Africa and its asexual
wild grasses. Homer scarcely knew it,
the Greek poets seldom mentioned
the kiss though it took the rest of Europe
by surprise. In Lapland
the kiss was the centre of gravity, you
planted it just below the navel where a pool
of sex-water lay. In Celtic tongues
there was no word for it and so I sat alone
in a farmhouse trying to invent
a name. The Welsh kissed
only on special occasions, at a game
called *Carousel*. Whenever there is rope-playing
there is also moonlight, and then one
came to me, shaped like a beet
or pear. Throughout East Asia
the kiss was unknown, in Japanese
literature pleasure was intense.
The kiss has always been alive
in the ravings of schizophrenics, reveries
of satyrs — a theta wave in the alchemist's brain.
During lovemaking the Tamils licked each other's eyelids.
I wish to speak of such tenderness,
the wisdom inherent in voluptuous acts.
In the light of Palestine
the kiss grew in the incandescent
spaces between olive trees.
Among early Christians:
of sacramental significance —

kiss the relic of a saint, foot of the pope.
In Rome the kiss was a sign
of reverence and so the erotic
possibilities did not become
flesh. Was it
the terrible kiss of God
that caused the virgins of Central Russia to lose
consciousness and turn into dock leaves?
In Borneo nose-pressing was the kiss
of welcome and of mourning.
Arabian deities
were easily uncaged
when about to receive kisses.
Powerful the impulse and yet the Chinese
thought it cannibalistic. Among the hill tribes
of India: olfactory, nose to cheek, *smell me*,
they said. Mothers of the Niger coast
rubbed their babies with their lips,
lovers did not. And the great unlit kiss
that feeds on mud at the bottom of the lake!
I wish to speak of the mammal's bite
and the hunger inside me, for every human infant.
Watch them. Their small fists
bringing each detail
up to their mouths.

Seventeenth Century

This time we discover ourselves dressed in the rough
nakedness of English peasants.
It must be dusk, that century of famine and plagues.
At the backdoor there's crying
in the beggar child's voice, dry bits
of hunger catch in the branch of an oak tree.
I don't recognize this room, its high ceilings
and rose wallpaper. Though the bed we've just enjoyed
is the antique we bought all those years ago
at a farmer's auction. Footsteps
down the hall and I know we've been waiting
for someone — a wealthy nobleman in knee
breeches, ruffled sleeves?
On a table by the window
there's a pitcher of beer, pewter plates
heaped with ox tongue, bread.
Knowing our hopelessness
has a kind servant set this cold meal?
I reach to cover myself with your shirt but you say, *no*.
Beyond the open window
stag and poacher are being driven
into the same trap, the orchard's shouting
something dazzling. Perhaps we are
waiting for your uncle, my brother, any man
with a plume in his hat and the heart of an executioner.
A cough, the turn of a doorknob.
When did we start thinking like this?

Pompeii

I have lost you in a portico where lovers once lay
side by side facing the mountain.
Today it is smokeless, covered in vines.
I climb staircases leading to winged women
carrying shields, sanctuaries set on high podiums.
With every step my feet remember catastrophe's weight.

The square is noisy with hawkers, the raucous
voices of moneychangers, but it's your breath
I want among the ruined columns.
This morning the Antiquarium is free of tourists.
I observe the casts of bodies, search
the saloons backwards the way I read a book,

right to left, knowing truth shows itself
in hollows: a young woman lying face down,
a dog twisting on its chain.
In the courtyard I stand on a raised gallery.
Perhaps you are in the vestibule
opening onto the Forum. There have always been days

of justice and injustice, the human heart on trial.
If you've passed through the House of Gladiators
there's no sign. Not even a circus fighter's
helmet rolls over the grass. Last night
in the hotel room we pushed the narrow beds together.
Almost two thousand years since a world

was obliterated beneath pumice-stone and ash
and still your fingers are legible on my skin.
At the road that forks three ways I call
your name. No smothering pall
and yet I am flanked by confusion:
tombs and mausoleums remind of what's known.

I offer nothing at the Temple of Apollo,
no fruit or jug of wine. What is passion
if not an endless excavation? And now I am
running, an animal who's caught the scent.
Oh marvellous dwellings of antiquity
with their spacious larders, two ovens

for baking sweet cakes, a peristyle for walking exercise
on rainy days! At last I find you in the summer
dining room — amphoras and grapevines —
reading a guidebook, map open on your knees.
And if beyond these frescoed walls
merchants haggle over the price of buttermilk or cloth

it is not our concern. Let Pan fight with Cupid,
Agamemnon sacrifice his daughter, there will always be
a drunken satyr sprawled beside the fountain.
Our time together will end too soon.
This is why I have searched the buried city:
there are ways of being we have not unearthed.

What I Remember from My Time on Earth

I wore an expensive shirt
taken from the body of a dead man.

Every marvel I'd been born to unfolded.
Light fell close to my head.

Beneath overcast skies I learned slowly.
A wolf clambered on.

I slept soundly
in the midst of a masked tribe.

A child carried a large platter.
After rain: the smell of wild roses

above the beach. I wore the wolf
like a shawl, its paws folded neatly

around my neck. Being in love
was like living under water.

I walked behind three children,
each one carrying a turkey

stuffed with bread crumbs and figs.
In the midst of the tribe

I moved toward a feast.
The smell of roasted meat,

the wolf sliding down my back, why
had I given them such a dangerous load?

Drop your platters, I shouted,
and the tribe rushed forward.

The children became one small girl.
I removed my mask.

The wolf fled with
the fattest bird in its teeth.

Annie Stays Out All Night with a Man Called Death

Death / Meanwhile, in a strange / Part of town
looking for / Someone with a bad cough . . .
— Charles Simic

I was standing at the corner
when he came out of the cathedral
drinking from a bottle of champagne.
He had that imperious swing that's almost a command.
I thought, well, some suave character
I'd seen on the stage the week before.

Lord knows what you see in him,
my sister said, and left for the station.

We lived in a boarding house.
A little cross-eyed disc jockey and his wife
slept across the hall. He waited on her
like a slave. When we passed them on the stairs
they always smiled, cryptic. Fools,
my sister'd hiss behind their backs.

In an oak grove the man pulled me down.
His asymmetrical eyes made me think
of my childhood — climbing trees, jumping walls.

The first pub opened. I dragged my fingers
through my hair. God, I was thirsty.

Lovesick again, my sister said later
when I stumbled in, coughing
and feeling something like pride.

But what kisses, I told her, what raw blue kisses.

Walk in the Broom Stand

After dinner, a pause outside the Greek restaurant.
I feel like someone else, snappy as the breeze.
Swing my head, imagine bobbed hair
wooshing past my chin like a little cape.
Across the street in the park
Scotch broom sweeps a hillside.
A few shrubs sailed round the horn
in the nineteenth century, only three
survived the first planting.
It won't leave, this feeling
I'm someone else, more gentle or more
aggressive. *It grows over Northern Europe,*
I continue, sounding more like
a botanist tour guide
than your wife, *but there*
it's kept in check by a whole host of pests.
And now I feel unpredictable, the kind of woman
who'd give some secret part of herself
then snatch it back. Exasperated,
would you stomp away from such a woman?
Or would you take her hand, walk into the stand
of late summer broom — every wildflower
choked out, nothing alive
but the orchard grass beneath you?
Would you accept as your own
each of her small, selfish acts,
ask her to accept each of yours,
dried pods bursting open like coiled springs?

A Strange and Terrible Thing

This is the dream: I'm making love to a dog.
And though I'm troubled by the canine
features of my desire
I choose to ignore
what I know in my passion —
that our coupling is a strange
and terrible thing contrary to nature.
And when the dog rises up on its hind legs
I see it has the body of a man.
Though in every other sense
it's still a dog —
tail and fur and long, smooth snout.
The act is without cruelty; we meet
halfway, standing upright, face to face.
And afterwards I feel no shame; I understand
the dog is a vessel containing the joy and sorrow
accumulated in a lifetime. And I want always
to hold in my mind the human
beauty of the dog's face
so I draw a thick frame around it —
a train window retreating into the distance.
And later I wake
aching with a loneliness I had not known
before the dog came to me
in the night and pressed its body
against the dark animal of mine.
All day I walk in dumb circles
remembering how the dog bent me down
with paws I can only describe now
as the intelligent hands of love.
And here, in this exhausted light,
I call and call out — *Oh core of my heart* —
words that mean nothing but
obliterate all else.

The Summer the Marriage Comes Apart

Hot sheets in the wind, your hands moving down.
How long have they moved this way,
as though they understand something's died?

Beside the bed — two mangoes and a jug of ice water.
After we roll apart I step onto the balcony
thinking: so that's what it's like
making love to a man
whose soul is not in it.

The lake is loon-filled, fluted with cries.
Out here the mosquitoes avoid my blood
as though I've got the plague.
A saucer-white moon breaks
into the mess of reeds.

Beyond the row of blue spruce a man keeps shouting —
love, you say love, well sweetheart I ain't
seen any of that around here for thirty years.

He's drunk, you call from inside and begin
to dream: dancing, we're in step
at last, and then I'm dancing
with a man wearing a shirt
the colour of eggplant, a Latin band
plays tango after tango, almost midnight
and the crowd's wild as Mardi Gras.

And what do I dream?
That you are kissing Ineke,
my mother's neighbour. That her husband,
the landscape gardener, is sitting on a sofa
gripping the hoe across his knees.
Good God, look at his face, I say,

pulling you toward the front door
where our shoes are cutthroat
trout swimming just below the surface.

Soulless, you say, reaching into the murk.
Soulless, I say, lifting out mine.

The Picnic

I walked down an old logging road
at the end of June. By then only cattle
passed through that part of the forest
on their way to a pasture that opened
among the trees like a blast
of goodwill. I was fifteen and carried

a sketch pad hoping to spot a deer
grazing on anything, but spied instead
a man and woman picnicking on a bluff.
Their complete absorption absorbed me
completely. From where I stood
it seemed their lips not their words

held the meaning, their conversation
would continue for weeks or months if only
the sun would stay high. What fixed me
to that place was the sound of high
wind like the sound of rushing
water, my sudden aloneness

and the fear I'd never get past it.
I rested against a moss-covered stump
and when I opened my eyes they were still
talking and then the man shuddered
as though a terrible memory
had come unlodged. Have I mentioned

they were naked, that the woman reached over
and comforted him with a tenderness
even I, shameless voyeur, had to
turn from? A series of soft
blows to the heart drew me
back and back again to sketching

their profiles, and when
the woman knelt over the man the way
a carpenter will kneel in the shavings
at the end of the day — hands, breath,
a flawless plane of wood — I put down
my blunt piece of charcoal.

2

This Business of the Dresses

In the middle of dinner I guide my sister
into the living room and light the gas fire.
There is nothing I can say to comfort her
and so I say nothing about our father
or the reasons he had for dying. Instead
I tell her about the time our mother
took us on the bus to Eddie's,
a clothing store, long demolished, took
the four of us down the stairs to the children's
department, a fire-trap basement
crowded with circular racks.
It was July and our mother's nerves
glowed brilliant as the frenzied
buzz of low, neon lighting.
In the change-rooms we pulled dress
after rustling dress over our heads,
smashed crinoline slips against
our bodies as though anything
so extravagant could ever be tamed.
She had so little money, I remind my sister,
*how had our mother managed to save enough
for those dresses?* She shakes
her head, she doesn't know how, or that
the weeping has left her body and stretched itself out
in front of the fire. This business
of the dresses glares so fiercely
beneath a distant sun it is difficult
to see us walking home on sidewalks that spread
beneath our feet in waves of blue camus.
When we come to a house floating above the grass
our mother stops
and digs around in her purse
for a key she cannot find.
We follow her, then, up the front steps.
Sometimes I think we are still there,
in that glassed-in porch, holding onto

our Eddie's shopping bags. I think our knocking
has awakened our father from a nap, that
somewhere on the other side
he is groping his way
through the wine-coloured light
of late afternoon, I think we are hot and thirsty
and still waiting for him
to let us in.

Bridlington

There was a time my mother was happy. She swears it. If I
think backwards I too will wake into that spiral of light
before I was born: my sister's not yet a year and my father,
just weeks out of police academy, rides a bicycle though the
streets of a seaside town, thinking this is just the beginning,
thinking there will be plenty of summers like this one. He
has no notion that life is more than a room at the top of a
lofty brick house.

Midday and my mother pushes my sister along the
promenade, past the pinball arcades to a bench where my
father comes for his lunch break. Sandwiches, oat cakes, a
thermos of tea.

During one of these picnics my father spots a young woman
lying on the beach, fully dressed, half in the water, half out.
She works on a farm and all the turkeys are dying. She
blames herself and wants death too but the tide keeps
retreating. While waiting for an ambulance, my father, not
knowing what else to do, kneels in the waves and massages
the woman's calves.

From a place beyond sirens and the ping of a thousand metal
balls he hears the hushed gobble of shadowy fowl, but what
grips him in the moment are the woman's legs, long and
shapely in stockings gritty with sand. *Like cold skin*, he'll tell
my mother later in bed, *like something alive that's already
begun to slough off the bone.*

Blue Magnolia

I found the baby beneath a pile of rotting oak leaves.
I'd been looking for my garden clippers.
Skin had grown over the places where her arms
had fallen off, they were seamless
as though the missing limbs
had never been. Finding her
armless was unthinkable, and yet she was
plump as an October apple.
As though mother birds
had been syphoning milk from cartons
delivered onto dewy porches.
I picked her up and realized
she was my own, I had given birth to her
one blue magnolia morning.
I remembered carrying her into the garden,
past the walnut trees, past the fish pond,
laying her on a blanket, but where
had I left her? How long
had she lived in mouldy darkness —
one week, two? My head was a tomb of dank air.
Back inside the house I never left her.
Soon she could roll onto her stomach, she
developed a swivelling crawl.
She kicked and cooed like any other
baby and when she lay on her back
her eyes moved in soaring circles.
I would like to tell you her arms grew back,
that hands appeared one morning —
dwarf fans waving through the air, I
would like to tell you fingers
sprouted from those hands
the way fingers balloon from rubber gloves
when you blow into their inverted,
pink digits.

Rifle Range

We live in the forest and fir trees
surround us like candles, their tips
graze the summer sky. On a rock
overlooking the valley I push my daughter
on a rope so long and thick
she could be dangling
from a piece of thread tied to God's finger.
All morning the branch creaks like a sorrowing bone.
Afternoons it's three miles of gravel road
to the mailbox at the highway's edge.
No one but us and so much time.
Today my daughter is wearing yellow velour shorts
and matching top, a strip of white tassles
cuts diagonally across her chest.
When she walks ahead, chin in the air,
she looks patriotic somehow —
one of those small baton tossers
marching at the front of an American parade.
At the rifle range we look over the fence:
one-dimensional men lined up side by side,
hearts pinned to their breasts, brazen as bull's-eyes.
Where are they, my daughter asks, meaning
the policemen who drive here
on Sunday mornings, the trucks and Jeeps
that stampede the field to powdered dust.
Moss perfects and slows our world.
Wherever we look, muscled trunks of arbutus
leap from the earth, a kind of
balletic orgy. It's true,
there are other forests but none
can rival in beauty the forest we walk through
when the day has become too much
for us, and the black outlines
of human bodies wait patiently
among the shade of a July afternoon
as though for a firing squad.

Shaky News

My daughter who fears earthquakes
performs thirty-nine rituals each night before bed.
In pony pyjamas she moves around her room

at the top of the house,
solemn as a priest swinging his censer.
Still she's not safe, still

this island lies close
to the boundary of two crustal plates.
She announces: *ninety-four*

already measured this year.
And it's true.
The seismic activity seems never to end.

At breakfast she reads the shaky news:
scientists predict the big one
could hit tomorrow

or it could hit in three hundred years.
If she plays three notes on her flute
will the intervals ease stress

along the fault lines? If she bangs
her tennis racket on the wall
will the double thud

prevent molten rock from welling up?
In the corners of her eyes
there are sometimes tears.

Twenty interlocking tectonic plates
floating on the earth's mantle are too much
for one girl. I stand in her doorway,

watching her spin a cardboard globe
thirteen times east, thirteen west,
as she drags an old hobby horse

across the carpet, seven times one way,
seven times back. No one knows
the precise effort involved

in holding up our crumbling lives.
Nightly she appeases the gods of sliding
rock mass. Against the skylight,

soft rain and I can almost remember
the birdsongs of spring, how once
her small body was lifted into my bed

where she slept supernaturally safe —
that disaster-free zone
between mother and father.

Tonight my daughter lies back exhausted,
crosses her chest twelve times and then
twelve more. In the corners of her eyes

there are sometimes tears.
It is too much for one girl.
The seismic activity seems never to end.

The Dress

I worked in a stenographer's pool,
seven hours bent over a typewriter.

Mindless work but I liked that about it.

I bought the dress
on a fifteen-minute coffee break.

Plenty of room to grow inside its full skirt.

It was 1977. I was hungry all the time.

The dress was white cotton.
It had spaghetti straps and fell
just short of the ankles.

There was an accountant
who liked to talk about poetry.

The other secretaries wondered but said nothing.

My mother left boxes
of baby clothes on the back doorstep.

Even the accountant couldn't tell
until the last month.

It suits you, he said, but I told him
I wanted to be myself a while longer.

My daughter is too much like me.
She does not give her love to what lies ahead.

If I saved things
I would have saved her the dress.

But then I didn't know, I just didn't know.

The Game

The children climb the apple tree.
In bathing suits they're grinning monkeys
posing for a photograph. I'm
on the ground struggling with the outside
tap beside the basement door.
The children are my younger sisters.
They're waiting for me to turn
the hose in their direction.
I twist the nozzle to its extreme position
knowing the force of the spray
will knock them from their perches.
My sisters love this
summer game; they scream and holler
and beg me to drench them again.
Years later they'll speak of my cruelty,
to my son they'll embellish
my sadistic nature. His clear
and trusting face will sicken
each time he hears the story
but he will never get enough
of those distant children
shivering in branches and helpless as prey.
And the one below in gumboots and garden gloves —
a demented firefighter blasting small bodies
as though they were flames?
He will adore her as he'd adore
any nine-year-old girl who holds in her hands
the sweet jet of power.
There is so much he can learn from her:
the tightness around her mouth,
the way she stands.

Giant Among Them

1

When we were children wading in the sea
one couple after another
arrived from Greenock to settle
in the summer houses along the beach —
sharp-tongued women whose husbands were not quite
uncles so we called them
by the names already pinned to their size
back in the old country: *Wee Billy,*
Wee Robert, Wee Jock. Men
who had to look up
to our six-foot-tall father.
With his thunderous laugh and great appetite
he was a giant among them.
What do you expect, they'd say,
the English didn't suffer during the war.
Standing beside them, we measured ourselves
against those stunted years —
air raids and rations, generations
of coal dust choking their lungs.
Your father grew up on a farm,
he lived the life of Riley,
Uncle Billy'd tease after a few pints.
And we'd dangle our feet over Fisherman's Wharf
waiting for the silver dollar
he'd slip us if we didn't disagree.

2

Our father told a different story.
How he picked potatoes till his hands bled,
as a boy how he dreamt not of sex or village girls
but of clotted cream, roast beef, and apple pudding.
And German pilots shot like pigeons

out of the Yorkshire sky.
Grateful men who worked alongside him
in the fields, their devotion to the führer now spent
peeling turnips, playing whist
with his older sisters.

3

Early July and that war's buried
on some distant beach. Our father
no longer hungers for anything heaped
on the plate of this world. At Witty's Lagoon
my sister and I sit on a log watching my son
skim his board through low tide.
Again and again riding the same narrow spit of sand.
I wince at his almost-nakedness — how thin
he's become over winter. My sister's eyes
reach as far as the mountains.
Our father's body, she says,
the famished frame of someone always looking
to the feast beyond.

Madman

For weeks he'd watched us skip at recess —
me and my sisters and some younger siblings
I didn't know we had. Somewhere
in Mexico and the lime trees were flowering.

When the noon bell rang
I made excuses — why the small ones
should stay inside and eat their lunches at their desks.

Behind the village fountain
he waited with his pistol.

The school was old, brick and marble.
Our teachers were invisible
or smoking in the staff room.

I understood someone had to die.

My sisters closed their spelling books
and put away their pencils.
I watched them disappear through swinging doors.

What happened then?
White-washed light broke in waves.
More than that, who could say?
Years ago our father had also become
a mixture of these things.

If I could have watched myself
pulling down the blinds in that classroom
I'd have seen an old, old woman
struggling to say a few words.

Deciduous saplings sprouted in the waste-basket
where last month's orange peels had decomposed.
The rotting smell made me think
of fish swimming into a pelican's beak.

I knew my time would come.

Eat up, I told the small ones
who shook their leafy heads.

The Fire

Three days ago this boy was suddenly too old for plastic
army men dressed in battle fatigues.
After dinner he hung around
the back steps, bored and indignant and
kicking up dirt: why couldn't he take the raft
he'd hammered together into the middle of the bay?
We were doing the dishes when he slouched in.
Could I dig a pit, put rocks
around it and build a fire?
We looked at each other.
It had been a wet summer so
we said yes to the fire and the great, green,
unignitable forest. For three days now
we've carried his meals out
to where he's hunkered down
at the edge of the pit in a derelict
lawn chair — an old man chewing tobacco
and staring at nothing. Each morning he breathes
fresh life into it and each night
douses it with water. He loves
its insatiable appetite, feeds it crumpled newspapers,
broken branches, he cares for this fire
as though it were a lame rabbit found in the woods.
Tonight the indistinct figure stabs at dying coals,
waves a glowing stick through the dark.
And what does he write across the sky,
what blackboard message
after childhood but before
girls dive into his eyes? So much
has been forbidden —
slingshots, firecrackers, deep water.
But for now he is motherless,
all crusty hair and sooty face, a cave-boy
entrusted with something
dangerous and
he will not leave it.

No Name for the Tree

Before turning out the light
I glanced at the magazine open on the floor.
The tree made me gasp the way trees
often do when you step back
into the glossy distance.
I got out of my pyjamas
and stood beneath its vegetable shape.
There was no name for the tree
though the sky was generic
in its grandeur and cumulous clouds.
I floated up into the network of green;
the birds seemed more themselves.
A boy pushed a girl on a swing.
His body kept rushing to meet the small of her back.
I will never know if their lives worsened like a rainstorm.
You have not asked about the dog
leaping at the girl's feet
each time she swung to the earth.
I stayed up there for as long as it took
to understand the theory that started the world.
Winter never arrived or if it did
it was brief as a shudder.
I will leave my heart out of it
though I give you the tree that stirs in my mind,
a tree so true to its sap and its roots
I have already begun to forget.

Old Friend

You are in Zanzibar when your old friend comes back
to life. His photo album
releases a swarm of fruit flies.
A baby is drawn from the sea, there's a fragrant musk.
Somewhere his children are cut-out dolls
with detachable robes. You ask
about his wife and his hand moves over
the island's undulating hills.
A slow gesture remembers the slave trade.
Now sit with him and drink sweet coffee.
The world and its palm trees
had almost forgotten him but not you.
See for yourself —
acres of cloves laid out to dry in the tropical sun.
He is taller than he was and there's a new thirst
in his eyes. He opens his arms
to rock the crying baby.
She closes like a bud against his chest.
All night you speak with such intensity
the tradewinds link up with your regrets.
You don't notice ships from Portugal and England
sailing away, their holds glutted with ivory.
It's a fine morning when he rises to go.
Wait, you call out sharply, knowing
you will never get the baby back.
What does it mean that he walks into the Indian Ocean?
He is your old friend and he turns
to give what he can — solace,
the husk of a coconut.

Letting Your Daughter Go

At sixteen she drives the family
car out of Sundsvall, speeding through Jämtland
and past the inland lakes. Highway police
try to flag her down but the plains of central
Sweden ripple behind, hot sheets in the wind.
For three days she drives
north, 1,500 kilometres from the pine bed
she's slept in all her blond life.
Her laminated licence is a piece of Arctic sky
pressed inside the pocket of her cut-off jeans.
In Kirkens she stops for a sandwich and Coke.
The shopkeeper nods her head, points
toward darkness and home —
turn around, go back, you're heading
in the wrong direction.
Bjorn Syversen, the jazzman's son,
has gone to follow the riff
his body plays on nights unblinking as this one.
He will drive until he finds a blue Volvo
hurtling past fingers of sea reaching into the mountains.
He knows your daughter has not misread her map,
she is not confused by constant daylight.
The midnight sun is her guide, it
draws her like a boy's warm mouth.
The sorrow and daylight are endless.
Like your mother before you
you lie behind heavy blinds
charting a passage along the northwest coast.
This epic journey!
It burns in her blood like gasoline.
The pure distance pulls her deeper into the white
light at the top of the world.

Three Days Before Christmas

You have a breath without pain.
It is called happiness.

— William Stafford

Three days before Christmas and a rock-opera
rendition of *Silent Night* was playing
on the car radio. Beside me
my son hummed along, his friends
slouched down in the back, their faces
vacant, just glad to be going
somewhere, anywhere, a rec centre
with a chlorinated pool. I was driving
past the sea wall thinking
I'd drop them off
then stop on my way home
for bagels and bananas when a hand
reached out of the sky and rested on my shoulder.
All was calm. I remember
the day was unseasonably mild, that sunlight
haloed the cherry trees
blooming too early along the winding
coast road, I remember liking
the rock-opera rendition of *Silent Night*, also
my son and his friends, the way
they hunched over the towels in their laps
as though the Christ-child himself
were jelly-rolled inside. All the same,
how explain that sudden peace?
I was conscious as a tree is conscious.
Like a stone I simply was.
And then the station-wagon was a riotous belly
emptying itself of eleven-year-old boys.
The hand lifted, the sky slammed shut.

I was myself again, a woman with greying hair
sitting in a parking lot
watching three boys swish down
a sidewalk in T-shirts and jeans so enormous
they might have been small,
fine-boned angels
shuffling toward
the bright waters of heaven.

The Meteoron

When my father died I climbed a steep climb.
I stood at the top of a pine-covered
mountain and watched the earth burn.
The sun lit up pilasters and menhirs
and I knew then why my father
had gone to the monastery
perched on the magnificent rocks —
to preserve his solitude,
for lack of any other solution.
In life he was not a holy man,
but in death he planted himself
at the top of a broad rock-shelf with no access
other than a ladder
only he could fold and draw up.
I shouted as far as the Pindus mountains
but he could not hear me.
Finally at peace, my father sang
as he hoisted up chickens and sheep,
buckets of water, his daily bread.
I watched him work his nets and winches,
remembering how the heft and weight of things
had always been good in his hands.
It's been years since he stole
like a monk into the *Meteoron*.
Don't ask me what it means —
the fantastic distance between heaven and earth.
Why we must face a surreal landscape —
needles and sugarloaves,
architectures of dizzying blue.
Go now to Trikkala, that city of antiquity
where the finest horses were bred
for their beauty and speed.
Do what you must with your father's death.
I have done what I could with mine.

Wheeling Through Tuscany

Last night both children dreamed
they flew to the same foreign country,
and the planes they travelled on
were so poorly constructed
they could look down between their feet
and see the world pass beneath them.
They woke broken-
hearted, longing to go back.
And their faces were uncertain
as though haunted by what they could now
only imagine — fields of sunflowers
and cyclamen. They stared
at the cereal soggy in their bowls and said,
it was green there, really green.
And what I want to know is
should we book a flight today, should we
travel to Tuscany now the children's inner lives
have spilled like Chianti into ours.
Small packs on our backs
should we rent bicycles and pedal
into that wet-grape darkness?

House

If that house had an erotic life we did not know it.
If its face was once beautiful
we did not mention
the day its teeth were removed
and its jaw forever altered.
We threw our voices down the laundry chute,
looked at each other and said nothing
about tumbling into the abyss. We couldn't fly.
Our descent was similar to that of the five green bibles.
We frightened ourselves
kicking inside its wide-mouthed chimney.
And when we tired, our bodies became pale
thoughts struggling through water.
Ours was a poetic hunger: the years
as crusts of dark bread and broken as Russia.
We made hard little fists in the bathroom
mirror and once I went down for breakfast
to find our mother in the alcove,
her hair a nest of wild bees. *Let's
not argue any more*, she said, *because
let's face it, no one's won an argument yet.*
How do you carry your losses except on your back?
And if we slept late that house spat us out.
We arrived at recess, confused, blinking
like traffic lights. Some things
are forgivable but that house was not one of them.
We got so far and then got stuck:
marine animals swimming out its bottom windows.
I stroked its doors as though they were old
sweethearts, I lied to the clocks, those cracked
moons of winter. I pushed my sister down the back steps
and said, *there, now quit your punching.*
We thought we could break
with that house as though with an enemy
but it kept coming back
in pornographic photographs —

a woman, circa 1923, stretched out on a velvet couch
wearing black stockings, a gold necklace.
Think about it —
there's something touching
about anything naked.

3

Walking Down the Staircase

He follows behind, all his mute passions
folded inside like sheet music. Too bad
summer's over, but it was beginning
to look like a rerun movie.
I roll up my sleeves and keep moving.
Out in front I hold a hand mirror —
a kind of torch to light the way.
Like the sky, his face is always changing.
Beyond his reflection, our younger selves
swim in a sea of chalky blue.
If I knew the phase into which
the moon has entered
I'd know why his words surprise like a bat's swoosh.
On the way down we pass huge circular windows.
Not much hangs on the walls
except black-and-white photographs.
Those and the cardboard fruit
children cut out of all the beautiful colours.
I keep thinking I'm pregnant.
If we could sit for a moment in the Penguin Café
I'd try to explain this overwhelming desire
to stop and make my body a home.
No one knows where these steps lead
except down
to the piano's last few bars.
His eyes are fixed on the back of my knees.
This is a good thing; it means the lines of poetry
scribbled inside my jeans pocket
have begun to ripen. He of course
has walked behind me long enough to know
there is no scrawl
I would not try to decipher, and anyway, who
can understand why
they're walking down a staircase
in boots meant for more rugged terrain.

Nineteenth-Century American Greenhouses

I turn the book's pages, not actually
reading, and then the words
begin to take shape — *tomato, onion, rose.*
I read of stacks of plate negatives
serving no purpose

until nineteenth-century nurserymen
used them to construct glass walls.
And then I am stumbling across memory —
you are above me, beneath me, it is
your astonished face

I've captured with a photographer's eye.
The river is brown, off with
our coats and though it's December
the taste of that first kiss
and the sun's freakish warmth

persuades us to pass from light
into shadow. Was it that day
or some other you first spoke
of the unsmiling soldiers
posed in full uniform? After

we'd kicked off our boots
that I heard of those glass
negatives bought after the Civil War?
Bought cheap and fitted side by side
in long wooden frames so that

for years afterwards
heat shimmered off acres of roofs.
Death feeding life, you said, *or something like it,*
the thought of those smoky faces
gazing down on the seedlings beneath them

so satisfied something within you
you wouldn't go near it, you'd
let it stand in your mind,
untouched as those boys
before their bodies collided.

In the Museum the Hominid Speaks to Her Lover

We have been reconstructed, you and I, bone on bone.
Heavy brows, quizzical expressions.
Slightly hunched, we are almost human.
Our long arms and short legs — what good are they?
We stand before a windless backdrop — acacia trees,
a shallow blue lake, tusked deer grazing on wild celery.

Your head's tilted as though you're listening
to the distant hoots of baboon. Can you
hear me or am I chattering to myself
as I often did when you left for days at a time?

Inside this glass chamber nothing to do but stare out
at the erect and hairless ones who walk past,
glancing in. At what? Our buck teeth, protruding jaws?
I know by their faces we are not beautiful.

Friend, in this late century there are words
I want to say, words our early tongues couldn't manage —
mahogany, laurel, wild pear, litchi fruit.
Names and more names that once stretched
from Kenya's sandy shores to the Atlantic Ocean —
mango, rubber, ebony, myrrh.

I don't know what to do with such words.
Should I husk or shell them?
Bite into them, crack them open like ostrich eggs?

Some say we spent our days jockeying for food
and rank and sex. Others, more romantic,
imagine us crouching in the mist,
sipping from tulip-shaped bromeliads.

They've given you a hollow club to hold, me an infant.
I am overwhelmed by their kindness.
Did they know I have been inconsolable
over the loss of this child?
That even my fossil remains have ached for him?

The night of his birth dim light filtered through a sky
of leaves, squirrels glided above us.
His hands were slight as shrews,
his cheeks, sweet as hamsters.

He died at the beginning of the wet season,
the mountains around us belching dark clouds.
On cool evenings we'd walk out, our primitive grief,
the phantom shape walking between us.

The experts have determined many things —
that we lived in moss-laden hagenia trees
but when the earth cooled and the forests thinned,
we travelled upright, in small bands, onto the savannah.

What they cannot know: our dreams by firelight,
digging nuts together in the shadow of Rusinga Island.
Memories like the slow vanishing of seeds and berries.
What they cannot know is that you and I
walked onto those sun-drenched plains hand in hand.
That we often stopped to lie together
in the boulevards of grass that wove between
the trees, our kisses long and deep and oh my special friend
how I have missed you these millions of years.

Days of Summer

1

I sat in a deck chair reading your letter.
A blue spruce interrupted.
I was a newly weaned calf
mouthing grass without knowing
what to do with it. We might have been
Jack and Jill as the Egyptians had written them.

2

I was alone in an attic bed.
Aquatic plants grew from the beginning.
Slept late despite the neighbour's
lawnmower, the rooster's crow.
The day wrestled itself
to the marshy ground.

3

Stars shot overhead.
We stopped the car and got out.
The sky was the purple of so many tongues
speaking at once. You stood in the middle
of that country road. My hands opened
wide as questions.

4

In late afternoon Tigris and Euphrates
appeared on the dock dressed in their wedding clothes.
They wore top hats and wrote their vows in clay.
Love, they said, *is bone-crushing work.*

5

Something shifted inside me.
I remembered what it was to fall
out of my language and into another's.
You had so many wives but I was not one of them.
I rolled my eyes as if to say.

6

The alphabet kept slipping eastward.
Inscribed on your cheeks were wedge-shaped marks.
The sun broke like dirt between my fingers.

7

Can symbols alone tell a story?
I paddled downstream in the opposite direction.
The canoe was leaking
and just one more reason
to sink the cuneiform moon.

8

A dog bounded in.
At first glance, a lion,
but of course this had nothing to do
with the jungle. And then
the wind picked up, my hair stood on end

9

No music at the piano, the drinks cut in stone.
My eyes open, you'd become
pure hieroglyph, a man in gumboots
wading through seven grains of light.

10

I pulled hard on the oars.
For a single evening I was proof:
the Lady of the Lake floats beyond the rushes.

11

On blocks of wood: a fox and rat,
their candlelit heads
bobbing behind.

Crow's Apology

You're flying above a rhododendron forest
when a voice says *You are Crow.*
Just like that
you begin to steal things —
a jacknife, cufflinks, rare
books, their spines flecked with gold.
Why descend
into petty thievery —
the brass button pinned to his
jacket, his wife's earring
as it rolls off the dashboard?
You know only
his mouth is a silver cup
you long to pour yourself into.
You drop to your knees
and drink with the honey-badgers,
the giant hogs who rush in
with their brilliant
tongues of thirst.
It doesn't matter who's watching.
Beneath his gaze
you snatch hubcaps, wedding ring,
shoehorn. And when he laughs
his teeth glint intoxication. If
you steal parts of him
you can't give them back — his kisses
like the wet wings of insects
fanning your face. Who can forgive you?
You see what you want
and though it's not yours
you swoop upon it.

Our Lives Together as a Small Green Book

I saw or thought I saw
    our lives together as a small green book.
        And the title engraved in leather
was *The Story of the Bee.*
    And your presence beside me,
        the shock of its familiarity,

rendered each word true. Earlier
    I'd been thinking of all the times
        we did not know what we wanted
from each other and so could not ask.
    While you slept I turned the pages
        until I arrived at the threshold

of a rustling, wing-lit hive, I went down
    to where the great, open vats
        are cooled by incessant currents
of air, down into the humming centre
    far from the diamond light that steals
        through the opening. I am speaking

of the holy of holies, of the twelve sealed
    palaces where the adolescent princesses
        wait for the appointed hour
wrapped in a kind of shroud.
    The book's water-stained covers
        had not been cracked in seventy-five years

and when they fell open they were
    wet leaves in my hands. It was
        past midnight and what was written
grew feverish as the spirit of the hive
    when it goes forth at daybreak.
        I wanted to reach into the swarm, emerge

with fistfuls, reach back to those prodigious
        summer days before I knew you, like
            ladling out roasted coffee berries,
bunches of raisins, corn.
        And when a dome more colossal
            than St. Peter's appeared before me

the geometric dimensions of your childhood
        moved through the waxen walls
            of mine, I could smell the honey
stored in cells and reservoirs
        flowing toward earth in embroideries
            of gold. For two hours the book exhaled

a balm of white clover as though it knew what it was
        to be tired of everything. A passing car,
            a few drops of rain. I closed the book
and slid down beside you. For a moment I understood
        it wasn't love that had made and unmade us
            all these years but something

inarticulate as the ether. I don't know when I slept
        or if I dreamt our union was unique
            and bewildering but when I woke
I woke to an unaccustomed stir: the queen
        and her acolytes, yes even the white nymphs
            to whom thousands of nurses minister.

The Place Where Souls Meet

They say there is an aquamarine room facing the river
where even the shadows have shadows, a sacred
site where bodies preexist and take
each other in, and this, they say,
is why we travel to distant countries:
to place our feet in worlds
where mythical beings spring alive.

Once I sat cross-legged in a school auditorium
and when I looked up I saw a boy
walk in through the exit door, his face
in the lunch-hour heat was a series
of marvels and signs. And when he moved toward me
through that wasteland of apple
cores and adolescence it was as though
he'd been moving in this direction a long while.
He spoke and I heard other voices —
familiar, remote — a lost language
where half-formed creatures
slipped through hanging gardens.

For years you have been my excavation, I
have been yours. Together we have
dug and tapped and sifted
through layers so that now sometimes
we break through these walls
with all their contradictions.

They say there are moments
when even the untrained eye can see beyond
memory into some other dimension
where heaven and earth give up
their secrets and mouths are simply
mouths that bless each other, and I do, I
try to bless you now with mine.

In the Hotel Room

It's true, we did that earlier, but this time
I want it slow. He's undressing,
telling me about the new, humane circus —
no tigers or bears. On the TV commercial
a zebra pranced around a ring
and he had to look twice —
its stride, comic as any clown's.

He pulls off his T-shirt and jeans.
Have I mentioned that tonight my skin's a fibre
I need his tongue to unravel?

He tells of the reporter who mingled
with the crowd asking parents how they liked it.
It isn't fair, a father complained,
my children will never see wild animals.
After all, said a mother, *I can't afford*
to send my kids to Africa, can I?

For a moment he stands in the pool
of his nakedness; this is perfect
animal grace, this I'll always trust as real.

When I was eight I went to the Shriner's Circus
with my sister. How bored we were!
By everything. Even the sequinned women
standing on the backs of rushing horses.
And when the elephants balanced
on their hind legs, forelegs perched on the rump
in front, when they threw back

their great grey heads, trumpeting
in loud unison, we were not impressed.
These were monkey tricks.

In the hotel room, the curtains are impenetrable
green, the carpet's a swamp feet sink into.

Tonight he holds this face in his hands and says
what he believes — that we live as we dream,
alone. I tell him I used to believe sex
was just a rung on the ladder
but now I believe it is
the ladder. Or is it
a watery descent, this journey the bodies take
deeper and deeper towards a beginning
where they recognize nothing,
not even themselves?

Letter in Flight

*Piano tuner missing over Pacific hanging from 32 helium
balloons.*
          — Japanese transport ministry spokesman

If I have ceased to trust words, what's to blame?
So long I've been riding this wooden crate,
poorly equipped and tossed
in the air like a buoyant cup.

The night before my journey our telephone
rang blue as your favourite shirt.
I stopped my ears, wouldn't listen
to coast guards or government officials,
their feet buried deep in the Kanto plain.

You were not watching when I lifted off.
A tangle of strings! I shouted to the crowd,
how pleased I was with this bird's-eye view.
And higher — the islands arcing northward,
the Roof of Hokkaido.

From you I took little.
Only the ricecakes you packed
in an old biscuit tin, the wool blanket
your brother gave as a wedding gift.

The balloons above are rotund angels,
each one's six metres wide.
You would think such lightness
could carry me across a thousand copper seas
and yet I've not reached California.

At first I waved my arms at sandhill
cranes, small aircraft, anything that flew
became a friend but now the sky's
too vast and I am lonely

for the beginning and end of a day.
For our daughter, the way she'd hold for a moment
a face in her hands. And you,
sweeping the porch
when I returned in the evening
with a bag of small hammers, my tuning forks.

Keiko, I forgive you everything.
For loving too much and then not enough.

On postcards I scribble short prayers
before dropping them into the waves.

The wind pushes like a hammock.

The world is a dark hood to pull over the eyes.

How Seldom and Like a Miracle

The summer before you left was the summer
men grew wings and swooped above the sea.
Soul-birds, we wondered, or children
of the hawk? At day's end
the sky was streaked canvas
stretched behind those nylon wings.
We walked the waterfront, past the dog-
people gathered around in their evening circle.
How seldom and like a miracle
love appears in our lives, we'd say, looking up.
There is that word.
All through August Francis Bacon,
the pot-bellied pig, trundled unleashed above the cliffs,
and each night the dogs lunged from commands
to yap at its bristled flanks.
We'd stop to watch the indifferent beast
root up the trampled grass.
It seems a dream now —
walking past that circle, the dog trainer
burning in its centre as question
after question regarding the nature of love
turned over in our minds.
That word again. How inadequate
its description when there is nothing
separate except the longing bodies.
Even now I make no sense
of your leaving or what led to it —
the dog-people shouting *sit, lie down, stop.*

Acknowledgements

I would like to thank the Canada Council and the editors of the journals in which some of these poems have appeared: *Arc, Border Crossings, The Carleton Arts Review, Event, The Fiddlehead, The Inner Harbour Review, Grain, The League of Canadian Poets: Vintage 93, 94,* and *96, Living at the End of the Second Millennium, The Malahat Review, Prism International, Room of One's Own.*

I would like to thank Jay Ruzesky for his words of support and advice at various stages of the manuscript's development. Many thanks also to Don Coles for editing the manuscript with humour and an uncompromising eye. Finally, I would like to thank Terence Young for everything. Poetic and otherwise.